SEQUESTERED SOLILOQUIES

Sonnets
celebrating the fourth centennial
of Shakespeare's sonnets

earl jay perel

Chestnut Hills Press, Inc.
a division of
New Poets Series, Inc.
541 Piccadilly Road • Baltimore, Maryland
MCMXCIII

This book is respectfully dedicated to my
very good friend and old college buddy,
Robert Muñoz,
in appreciation for all the kindness he has shown
me and all the help he has given me since my
return to California. Without his patience,
encouragement and assistance,
this small volume might never
have come into existence.

꙳ 𝒫 ꙳

𝒫REFACE

Anyone who loves sonnets, especially Shakespearean sonnets*, should thoroughly enjoy Earl Jay Perel's performance in this genre. From the Ovidian wit of "Zeus was such a bashing bore in bed" (p. 89) to the macabre sobriety of "I dreamt myself a corpse as cold as ice" (p. 84) these sonnets give voice to a rich range of mood and emotion. While nicely modulated, they articulate a passion both powerful and poignant, as exemplified by "A hollow echo whispers in my heart" (p. 43) and "She was the sweetheart of my tender years" (p. 53). Reading Perel is not unlike listening to Bach or Mozart, for these sonnets contain the formal beauties of the one and the melodic charms of the other. Furthermore, both scholars and others will delight in the resonances of earlier poets to be found in the quotes, near quotes, allusions, and references peppered throughout this sequence. When Hallam Tennyson, the poet's grandson, invited Perel to read several of his sonnets for the BBC, he wrote: "They contain a very high degree of competence and metrical skill but they challenge comparison with Shakespeare's almost too daringly—particularly the love poems." It seems that what we may have here is a twentieth century Elizabethan, a truly Renaissance man! And if all the world loves a lover, these sonnets should become the Bible of sweethearts the world over for centuries to come.

—*Joe Montalbano*

*While Shakespeare's sonnets were not published until 1609, it is generally acknowledged that they were written in the 1590's.

Table of Contents

❧ ❦ ❧

xi

SEQUESTERED SOLILOQUIES
earl jay perel

⚬⚬

Abide with me, Cyprus Aphrodite,
A humble poor Pygmalion suppliant
Beset by marble Galatea's flighty
Heart of stone. Hear this ardent mendicant
Whose urgent prayers request the magic touch
That carbonizes adamantine form
To living flesh; for if he's loved too much
His soul's been scourged by pain and purged by scorn.
Unlike almighty Zeus he can't regale
His simple self as husband, swan or bull,
Or golden coins. This hedgehog Homer pales
Beside such gods who find his paeans dull.
 Yet, to those few who see and feel what art
 Imagines he'll appear a beauteous bard.

⚬⚬

Alone upon the ego's shore of self
Each man becomes an isolated isle.
No voice reveals some hidden inner elf
Who's balm conceals extinction's vacant vial.
Do souls exist? Mind's solemn unct'ous urges
Imagine incarnations yet to come.
It dares deny death's dignifying dirges
And claims a future fate beyond life's sum.
Transcending life's bifurcating 'clusion
Merest matter enjoys a timeless span.
Is life or after-life the real illusion???
This befuddling puzzle baffles every man.
 If atoms are eternal why not will?
 A silent universe keeps its counsel still.

ᴥ ℮ ᴥ

𝒞an we experience another past
Yet once again??? Can ever fate rewind
Some former life, and have its memories last?
What mysteries lie within the human mind?
Can spirit etch the crevices of brain
With all its ancient subtle forms and feelings?
Can deepened recesses truly new contain
Passions past our nature found appealing?
The hollow in my heart resounds with echoes
Of some preclusive love, some precious soul,
Some prior being's presence it now decodes.
I know not whom: but how my heart does toll!
    In vain I search to find this sainted shade;
    The ghostly her who haunts my futile 'cade.

ᴥ ℮ ᴥ

ℋow came you by such youth beyond your years:
Where are those winkles that truly tell your age?
No crow's feet fault your eyes as with your peers,
Your form's as firm as any nubile page.
The *joie de vivre* with which you face each day
Inspires as much wonder as your mien.
Whence comes the energy that you display;
Has your body's inner clock just gone insane!
That playful sparkle in your gaze betrays
A lust for life experience's enhanced;
Which those of tender years but sober ways
Would never understand until they've danced.
    Combined with vim and mind still in their prime,
    Somehow you've kept youth's gifts well past their time.

ɔ⸱ℓ⸱ɔ

I'd half forgot the sound of sonnets past
Until her soulful eyes, enticing still,
Disturbed my dreams. Those words I wrote seemed cast
In granite then, not shifting sands until....
To hear her voice recite my lines again,
If only in my mind's, a bitter joy.
The wasted hours spent recalling when
I curse and bless, yet know I can't destroy.
If god or genie once could grant my wish
This fool would find the words he could not say.
My tardy tongue betrayed my fears of risk:
The jewel I lost's the cost my heart must pay.
   And now I long for Lethe's kindly kiss:
   Her gracious gift, forgetfulness, is bliss.

ɔ⸱ℓ⸱ɔ

My inner eye and outward orbs engage
In civil war upon my tortured mind.
For thoughts of you command my mental stage
And leave my ocular responses blind.
I dote upon your image rendered there
And often miss what lies before my view.
Why do you cause my heart such cruel despair;
And rob my outer world of all its hue?
Your charms are such that even in my dreams
Just being there with you is better than
A physical reality that seems
A barren place of insubstantial sand.
   The joy your presence brings is such a state
   That kings would give their crowns to share that fate.

The paradise in hell's the hell in heaven;
There are some minds in which the two do meet.
The pain in ecstasy's the holy leaven;
It's there the darker Eros has his seat.
It's more than merely joy an sorrow joined;
It holds us in its grip by hidden roots.
It's something that we sense deep in our loins;
The woeful words we use betray its truth.
When consciousness becomes a typhoon tidaled
Its vertigo sends our senses reeling.
All existence is then enhanced unbridled;
Metamorphosed by this mystic feeling.
    The self dissolves with every quaking spasm,
    Which then begins to bridge our being's chasm.

Those fools who doubt the flesh's resurrection
All gasp to gaze upon the lovely face
That launched a thousand ships in Troy's direction
To claim again her beauty, charm and grace.
Or is it magic that's preserved you whole
Through all the centuries that passed since then.
Who granted you the gift to keep your soul
In one immortal form 'till God knows when.
To claim my words will do as much is vain
For poetry lacks the power to preserve
What's more than thought, though memories remain
And pass to future minds some small reserve.
    Thus those to come may learn to ruminate
    Upon this image others emulate.

Ungathered rosebuds will wilt in record time;
Why leave them then to Death's too eager jaws?
Enjoy them now in this their proper clime:
A garden or a graveyard—the choice is yours.
Should virgin chastity still be your end
Then enter in a convent where the care
Of virgin souls has nuns to superintend
Their safe retreat from temptation's snare.
Sleep's senior partner is quite patient there
Because he knows your choicest parts are his.
An intact maidenhead's his richest fare;
A treat that's much too fine for him to miss.
 This second self of sleep has brought to bed
 Uncounted virgins to rest among the dead.

We never understood what grown ups said
About someone we'd never see again.
What does it mean to say that someone's dead?
How does it feel to know that gnawing pain?
They tried to comfort us with some surmise
About an after-life where souls live on:
Which we believed because we thought them wise;
And felt relieved about the one who'd gone.
We're now adults with minds mature in doubt,
And so unsure about the place we'll go.
But when another goes we still cry out,
And tell our children what we cannot know.
 Yet when that debt comes due we're bound to pay
 Some ghostly clown may come and claim our clay.

so ℓ so

*W*hat light illumes the heart if not the spark
That fancy fuels when beauty such as yours
Enthralls the mind and banishes the dark:
Your blessed freshness excites my soul to soar!
Both shy and pert, then innocently coy;
You'd turn a cynic a consecrated saint.
The whimsy of your wit's a charming ploy
Of tantalizing thought that's rare and quaint.
This vacillating vacuum's prone to pride:
Its vain pretense is but its ego's mask.
Imagine then how much you've mystified
The rigid righteousness it's deemed its task.
 Your love has taught my frozen heart to flow,
 And left my melted ego all aglow!

so ℓ so

*W*hen this crafted clay becomes a corpse
Cremated back to dust and brittle bone,
Leave what's left out where the weather warps;
Scattered far and wide to points unknown.
I'll have no further need of these remains:
Why then should they be boxed and eulogized
In finely chiselled stone that fails to frame
My fate: such foolishness is ill advised.
Should there be some who still may hold me dear
I hope their memories bring nought but joy.
I only ask of them that they adhere
To my belief that souls are redeployed.
 If energy and matter play their game;
 May not our souls and bodies do the same?

18

so ℰ so

*Y*our woman's heart's the holiest of grails.
To earn your love's the noblest of quests.
To win your hand would cause a god to quail.
By grace alone some knight might yet be blessed.
Majestic kings may come to pay you court;
To offer all the treasure due a queen.
Such worldly wealth's oft given for the sport;
Royal passions oft may prove a love that's lean.
Dub me your knight I'll face the fiercest fire
To conquer any doubts your heart may hold.
A dozen dragons' belching flaming choir
Can't keep me from your holy grail of gold.
    My sword's the finest steel Damascus forged:
    I swear I'll slay your dragons all, by George!

so ℰ so

*A*bout a dozen decades might suffice
To find the words to tell you how I care.
At present all I know is there's no price
I would not pay, or deed I would not dare,
To keep your love until the day I die;
And hopefully in heaven ever after.
My breathless heart now hangs upon you sigh,
And all my being leaps to hear your laughter.
Could I explore a universe of earths
I would not hope to find your like again.
I fear my love must prove of lesser worth
Should it be judged by merit in my pen.
    I swear I'll never leave your loving bed
    Until my mortal flesh is cold and dead.

Bare ruined choir—a sparrow's lonely haunt—
Whose rusted rows of pipes have lost their voice.
A vacant nave of pillars stark and gaunt
Where Bruno's vow has stilled the songs of Boyce.
That crowning rose, since robbed of all its hues,
A web of stone that skeletons the sky.
Those glories etched in glass are vanished views
Of martyrs who found faith to dare to die.
The marble altar's bereft of relics blessed;
Beneath the chapelled apse's a crypt of tombs.
What ecstasies excite eternal rest
Among these Christian saints who sleep in ruins.
    No bells above ring out Te Deums' toll;
    His sacrament of grace has lost its soul.

Carthusian quiet mutes my monkish muse;
He counts his beads this cloistered celibate.
Preferring prayer to poetry, meet for pews,
He minds the mass and bids Parnassus wait.
The mystic's vows and visions stone his heart:
This world of wit, will, wealth and women taints.
Contritely lighting candles, love and art
Eschewed, this holy Homer mimes the saints!
Unfrock this folly, these orisons and odes,
These chanting scrags canonicals of doom.
Love and craft create (the cross corrodes)
For poems redeem their pledge in runic bloom.
    Should sterile stones entomb this teeming tongue
    Your being's birth and beauty sleep unsung.

❦

I was a lad of ten and little more,
And gave my premier speech with tearfilled eyes.
I spoke with all my heart, but don't recall
The topic of my talk that won the prize.
To us our white-haired teacher seemed real old,
Like all our teachers she was often harried.
We knew she always had a heart of gold,
And used to wonder why she never married.
Once she told of when she was our age,
Her dad recalled the days of Sherman's hell.
Her Georgia folk still felt both hate and rage —
T'was then we learned she'd been a southern belle.
    She held my hand and said I was a charmer;
    Envisioning me a knight in shining armor.

❦

My lagged lines all limp across the page
In sullen solitude and silent dread.
Unwanted refuge from another age
They've lost all hope of ever being read.
They know themselves the ghosts of ancient tongues;
An older english now no longer heard.
The freshness of their form's completely wrung
So dry it's nought but dust encrusted words.
The magic of their metaphors is gone
Beyond the after-life some words enjoy.
Their meaning's memory loosely lingers on
Unless they're newly coined and re-employed.
    What words am I to use to sing your praises:
    They're each a Lazarus your love up raises.

My winter world had never known such bliss
Until you came and kissed me with such passion.
My heart still marvels at my mind's abyss
Before you taught me love's more recent fashion.
Your Tantric talents make our bed a shrine
Where Buddha meditates in calm repose.
Our naked souls now quietly recline
In yoga's peace to which this frantic rose.
That frenzied form of love I knew before
Has lost its lush appeal. Its anxious haste
Was just another form of sexist war,
But I've since learned it was a total waste.
    You've taught me all the joys of love's true art,
    And given me a much enlarged new heart.

Suspicions, doubts, and fears destroy all hopes
Of lasting love. True love depends on trust
That frees the heart, and leaves the heart a scope
As boundless as a sphere. This speck of dust:
This atom self may then encompass all
The universe, and time eternal too.
This new expanded self's pleased to give all
Its self and all it has to one who's true.
But once the worm of mental reservation
Eats its way into the heart then love becomes
A case of quid pro quo's anticipation:
It can't survive this count of matching sums.
    Love's not based on gifts, or gold, or gain:
    Love does more than share; it gives in joy and pain.

The phoenix of my dreams has always been
That ancient Helen of Homeric fame.
Another Faustus Lucifer may win,
I long to learn his dark alchemic game.
If poetic praise were half as potent
As any incantations from his book
I'd raise a host of Helens to augment
Those loves whose pleasing magics all mistook.
Their false infections always failed to last
Beyond the passions that they first inspired.
For once the fever that I felt was past
My heart was cured of whom it had desired.
 I know my secret longing's no thing of pride.
 Someday I'll find my Helen—or loose my hide:

ჯ ℰ ჯ

The truth of love, as pure as soft white snow,
May flow from soul to soul as falling flakes
To form in perfect crystals and calmly make
The heart it dewy kisses gently know.
Such love my heart embraces, love to grow
Upon thy heart as crystal lace, to wake
Within thy soul a feeling to forsake
All else save me; my love is thy repose.
And yet my humble soul so lacks the grace
To merit thee I dare not hope so much
As press thy hand. My tranquil love is such
That in thy sleep, unknown to thee, I'd trace
 This tender sign to lay upon thy face:
 A kiss as gentle as the snow's soft touch.

Those fools who want a virgin every time;
They value woman as they value things.
They think her tempting part's their private mine;
Her heart as well is meant to soar and sing.
For them the words of love are just a ploy
To gain their way with those their flesh desires.
They've little care to even share the joy
Their hungry selfish passion may inspire.
May not a woman also taste the wine
That love ferments in humans mind and soul.
Must not a woman learn those arts sublime
That spice the act of love however droll.
    My wish for those who only want a virgin:
    When life's at risk they get a first time surgeon.

What quiet queries pass between our hearts
While we politely pass the time in talk.
Our conversation's calm's a crusted bark
Upon the pulp of meanings instincts stalk.
Unplighted souls are eager to explore
Each word we voice so weighed with vortexed sense.
Unconscious urges' intonations score
Our anxious thoughts' whirlpool altered tense.
The searching vertigo our flesh endures
Twixt truth and ruth in passion's ebb and flow's
A teasing test that may in time insure
A life enriched with love's eternal glow.
    Thus tone and undertone create the balance
    That joins our minds in ego's binding valence.

Abstain from love until a riper age
When feelings in your flesh become so strong
They tell your heart it's time to heed their rage,
For lyrics in your soul must find their song.
When Eros finally has you in his powers,
And everything inside has turned to flame,
Your life will be a host of anxious hours
To find a mate with whom to play his game.
Yet love is something more than mere desires;
True passion burns the ego to a crisp.
It's a heaven found down in hell's fires;
All else is nothing more than will-o'-wisp.
    And should you dare deny this deeper truth
    You prove yourself a person without ruth.

Drink deep from Eros' fountain, for its springs
Intoxicate to madness modest lovers
Who seek to only sip the joys it brings:
Beware the passions Cupid's trials uncover.
Once damned by this addiction no one's free
To taste more sober pleasures however pure.
It's small imbibers pay the highest fee
To find some antidote in hope of cure.
But those who down their draughts complete and cool
Have learned to cede their hearts in finding bliss.
In passion's cause they're consummated fools
Who's world's well lost for a lover's kiss.
    Their's becomes a universe of wonder;
    Each time they're struck again by Zeus' thunder.

so ℓ so

*G*o 'way! Go 'way! You don't, you can't exist:
Unfounded fancy's figment you're too unreal.
Who conjured you to tempt me in this tryst
Imagination's worked my will to yield.
Each rendezvous we share's a dream-like state
That's too intense by far—it can't be true.
Crowned with nature's nimbus by teasing fate
You're sure to prove illusion's ingenue.
Inured to love's uncertainties I laughed
At trusting hearts. Yet now I pray you'll prove
An ever fixed star who guides my craft;
The faithful compass course to lasting love.
    Allay my doubts and fears: come grant your gift.
    Alas! Love's guillotine is sure and swift.

so ℓ so

I watch the moon arise night after night,
Each eve a brighter fuller orb than last.
The more it floods both earth and mind with light.
The more my heart must wane because it fasts.
I waste away the hours 'till the morn
With loving thoughts of you that torch my soul.
Those lucky men condemned to die at dawn
Are spared repeated nights that take this toll.
These constant vigils have turned me pale as ghosts,
My flesh now looks as lifeless as a corpse.
My martyred heart's upon a rack that roasts;
Reduced to hell my being's numb and torp.
    You hold the pardon, if only you'd relent;
    What must I do to win your heart's consent?

Ironic hope to long for human love.
Is nothing nobler? The grace of God perhaps.
The saintliness of service 'till blessed above.
Are faith's illusions false though fearsome traps?
Greatness. Glory. Heroic enterprise!
A valiant deed's the vanity of kings.
The world of lettered study, learned, wise.
Ivy's halls and honors are tinseled things.
The gift of genius, of molding matter,
Be it pigments, poetry, song or marbled stone.
Alas! All such soon serve as critic's chatter.
Where's that one eternal task to call my own?
    Life's lessons leave a fairly simple goal:
    A faithful mate whose magic sparks my soul.

I've found Elysium abides within your bed:
The arts you practice there perplex me still.
Your sweet surprises embellished in my head
Have nightly robbed me both of heart and will.
Loath to become involved you seemed a light —
How shall I say it? —a safe affair.
I even hesitated from fear I might
Cause this fresh and eager child to care.
To think I had my doubts about your charms!
You see at first I found you rather plain,
But once I met enchantment in your arms
I knew my soul would never be the same.
    You've taught me not to judge by looks alone;
    For one must read the text to learn the tome.

My late exhausted worlds of former loves
Are now a host of urns that haunt my heart.
Each holds a dune of ash from passion's stove,
The coke that stoked my humble kiln of art.
These spheres were souls I never meant to mar;
Our hearts were bonded so we were one mesh.
And now I bear the wounds, the hidden scars:
With each I'd scorched my oft' excited flesh.
There's justice in these self-inflicted brands;
For each is now a stigma of my sins.
Before the bench of Fate alone I stand —
My punishment's the lack of common kin.
    This donkey froze between the bales of hay:
    He could not choose, and starved right where he lay.

Select some younger swain to be your lover!
Some handsome giant to fill your nights with joy???
Experienced maturity uncovers
Your way to womanhood more sure than boys.
You dote upon Adonis: your being yearns
To recreate his many manly charms?
No roguish Quasimodo, whom passion burns,
Shall ever steal into your heart and arms!
Sweet virginal romantic, youth reveals
You've easily confused desire's urge
(And childish adulation's false ideals)
With love's affectionate and lasting surge.
    Your heart's the magnet needle of your mind?
    You'll not endure my Faustian designs!

The pleasures of the bed take psychic form
To stir our souls with love's most secret truths.
A night of loving leaves our being warm
And calms our mind with quiets that most soothe.
Orgasmic climax shocks us to the core
And magnetizes all emotion's range.
It polarizes egos to explore
The other sex's feelings that once seemed strange.
Both male and female blend to form a whole
That soon transcends our sense of either sex.
In time we're fused together soul in soul;
And thus one will is all we have to flex.
    No wonder that we seek such consummation:
    Compared to this all else is pure damnation.

≈ ℓ ≈

The universal urge all nature shares
To procreate inspires inner joys
That far surpass the sorrows, doubts and cares
Of parenthood. The bonds that life employs
To make us one in mind, and heart, and hope
Are worth the burdens they've sometimes imposed.
With love we can do more than merely cope:
We can enrich our spirits 'till life's is closed.
Now join with me to undertake this task;
Its sacred nature proves our days are blessed.
I know of nothing finer to give or ask:
Love springs eternal in the human breast.
    This gift of tenderness that's touched our life
    Would join our eager hearts as man and wife.

☼ ♪ ☼

Though mine is but a very meager gift
It's been a consolation all my life.
My trusted confidant, these sonnets, lift
My soul. They comfort me as would a wife.
The sense of purity a poem inspires
Is absolution from any guilt or pain.
A paper priest's all confession requires:
I find there's no cathartic quite the same.
Add then the debt of honor that they pay
To all the sonneteers I emulate.
How oft' my words were theirs I cannot say —
You see I've borrowed freely from the great.
    The life we live within ourself's more true
    Than any that appears to other's view.

☼ ♪ ☼

What rage is this that ravishes my heart,
And turns my tongue a traitor to my pride.
What dreams are these that wake me with a start
To tell me truths my psyche sought to hide.
What shapes are these that steal into my mind
To act out fantasies that seem obscene!
Are these the hidden hopes my id kept blind
Because it knows I'd find them all unclean.
Confused I long for solitude to give
Reflection to my troubled thoughts or you.
I can't believe my soul is just a sieve
For lustful appetites to pass on through.
    Can love that's fair be formed from all that's foul:
    Should this be true what can we disavow?

⁕ Ƈ ⁕

With my Socratic face I stand in need
Of Shakespeare's magic to move a woman's heart.
No star-crossed hero confident to plead;
Too oft' I'm forced to play the comic's part.
With nonsense, nuance, innuendo, jest;
In time I turn her secret thoughts to love.
When resistance weakens this welcome guest
May mount her throne of Venus, triumphant Jove.
But once I wonder who's seducing whom
That ugly worm of doubt destroys it all.
No Hamlet e'er escapes his destined doom;
The hemlock in his heart brings on his fall.
    My restless longings always turn to rust,
    No love can last beyond its time of trust.

⁕ Ƈ ⁕

Accept my silence as an act of awe;
No words can tell the wonder that I feel.
My mind's a haunt for formless thoughts of straw,
The cacophonic rests that score my peal.
In vain I search for words my untrained tongue
May voice in hopes they might express my soul.
Our language lacks the means—it leaves unsung
This love that sparks emotion's magnet poles.
If you've the woman's wit to read my eyes;
To sense the song that stirs my racing pulse.
If you've the heart to catch my heart's surprise...
A miracle's my need and nothing else.
    How can I ever hope that you'd succumb
    To one who's proved a dunce both mute and dumb.

And still you have those sonnets that I wrote!
It must be centuries since last we met.
As I recall they're not a thing of note:
I'd be embarrassed now to have them read.
I readily admit they were sincere;
You touched my heart as no one ever has.
Each epistle, for that's what they all were,
Bespoke a love that no one could call crass.
You know the passion that I felt for you
Was more than just a burning of the flesh.
Our souls were mated then, our bonds were true:
Whatever happened after our love's still blessed.
    All of these are yours? What a charming brood.
    You always were bewitching when in the mood.

Be now the bud that comforts my old age,
A rose in winter's cherished all the more.
Since soon I'm due in Being's second stage
Beguile my heart awhile as loves of yore.
Though past the state where passion burns the soul
I still can feel affection's tender touch.
With less an urge than sparks the lusty foal
I yet have gifts to please a heart that's lush.
Your sylvan charms shall grace my silver nights
As virgin snows that shroud the sleeping earth.
Fear not the dawn that brings my final rites;
It comes to prove my true and fullest worth.
    Help me complete the cycle of my years
    In calmful joys we'll share with cheerful tears.

Compared with you poor Helen was a hag.
The Greeks and Trojans both would never fight
Their futile war o'er such an ugly nag
Had they but seen her beauty in your light.
As for Circe: she'd turn all men to monks
Had they but known your charms for just one night.
Her enticements would seem the same as skunks
Had Odysseus enjoyed your sweet delights.
As for Dante's Beatrice, Petrarch's Laura,
Sidney's Stella, and poor Shakespeare's lad:
None can hold a candle to your aura:
For you alone have made the muses mad.
    Of womanhood you are the paradigm
    Of pure perfection to be gloried in.

I long to kiss the roses in your face,
To raise upon your lips a holy shrine.
With these enchanted kisses I would trace
A sanctuary against the rage of time.
The heart is but the hearth where Eros burns:
A tabernacle wherein love abides.
There let me lay a garland—it's all I yearn:
There rests the Host who vanquished mortal tides.
Life becomes eternal when kindred souls
Embrace upon this altar of devotion.
Once vowed to Venus hearts shall always hold;
Her elixir's a true alchemic potion.
    Come: let us down the draught, this magic drink —
    Let's sink in ecstasy 'till we no longer think.

ॐ

I've fumbled through the fog of this existence
In search of....sometimes I wonder what.
Admittedly I may have lacked persistence,
And rarely been quite pleased with what I'd got.
How oft' illusion masquerades as love;
How oft' the round of romance leads to sin.
How oft' I felt I'd never have enough:
How oft' the pleasures of the bed wore thin.
Though small my realm I monarchized awhile;
But petty powers left a placid taste.
Like any other villain I learned to smile,
While within I realized it's all a waste.
    Not that I'm bitter: but really can it be
    The fault's not in my stars: the fault's in me.

ॐ

No buds burst forth upon my barren bark;
A sullen spring ill apes the winter's chill.
Seams of snow gleam crystalline and stark
To limn the blossomed earth that beckons still.
Alas! my seedling time has long since passed;
Death's solemn sanctities sequester thought.
A darker fate may set my future's task
To make amends for wrongs I may have wrought.
What quirk of Ceres etched your form and face?
Your beauty swirls the sap in sleeping roots.
Your Phoenix powers promise gifts of grace;
Both bark and branches blush with tender shoots.
    But once to feel Venus' sweet infection
    One eag'ly seeks Eros' resurrection.

Our youth was green with summer's innocence,
That zenith time of dreams, and trust, and hope.
How dear the teasing was; the shy pretense:
Demurely loving in bold poetic tropes.
My sonnets then were each a sweet bouquet
Of verbal roses; fourteen to the bunch.
A kiss rewarded each 'till nature's play
Became intense: it struck us as some trunch.
Those tender truths naivete inspired
Became the cairns that marked our kindest hours.
Alas! The fruit the tree of knowledge briers
Bore not the rose of love's most magic powers.
 Though I may swear that I'm the one to blame;
 I curse the kiss that brought us bitter shame.

The grains within my glass are all but through,
Though those to count remain a mystery.
Had I Sahara's sands they'd prove too few,
As would the drops that fill the wine dark sea.
My appetite for life exceeds all measure
What ere the Janus risks that jeopardize.
Finite time's the thief that turns haste leisure
In grasping every second left to prize.
Death's auditors decree the date we sail
Beyond the bar that harbors hungry life.
What lies behind's an 'oft told idiot's tale;
Ahead's oblivion's end of hopeful strife.
 I'd heed Death's call had I but half the will;
 Demonic clouds of doubt consume me still.

so 🦢 so

The praises of my pen are all pretense:
How can they qualify to paint you fair.
They shame me so I fear I give offense
By sending them to you without repair.
They can but show the limits of my skill
Because my tongue is dumb without my muse.
But then my muse confessed his voice is still
Because he can't improve on nature's hues.
For only nature has the skill to paint
The beauty it alone can bring to life.
What artist dares to offer a complaint
Against the gods, thereby inviting strife.
    Yet I would dare to challenge all the odds
    If I could paint you as did nature's gods.

so 🦢 so

Were I to sit upon the muses' mount
I'd owe my throne to you; to you alone.
Your love's become the center, source and fount
Of all my thoughts. My mind was sterile stone,
But struck by you a waterfall of words
Gushed forth! Their flow informed the images
That turned to song my soul's too sour curds.
Now surpassed the muses hide their visages!
Not even Moses could have done as much
To bring to life my laggard muse's voice.
I'm sure you have our Christian Savior's touch
To change aquatic drink to wines of choice.
    Your loving's magic's made my mundane sonnets
    A verbal necklace formed of heart-shaped garnets.

Who bid some specter sneak into my soul
And mirror forth affection's fantasy
Where you are cast in Cleopatra's role
Adoring me as mighty Anthony.
Where I forgo the majesty of Rome,
A forfeiture unworthy of your love:
Where widow's mites, whose value lies alone
In being all I have, becomes a trove.
What facts betray these phantoms? Cold and cruel
Reality is but a lie compared
To fancy's fruits and inspiration's fuel
When hearts accept in faith what love's declared.
    Though some decry such shades as empty schemes
    None can deny the deeper truth of dreams.

Before we met I was a fallow youth
Who thought to conquer Cupid with his wit.
In love with love I never knew the truth:
Alas—I've learned I was a hypocrite.
The passion that you've planted in my heart
Bears witness to the worthless trash I wrote.
Love's not the place for logic like Descartes';
Nor for the bleatings of a bashful goat.
Those falser feelings I've found were merely glee
Because my selfish longings seemed so true.
The sense of wonder love's instilled in me
Has changed me mind and heart because of you.
    The love you've shown me has taught the blind to see:
    This foolish phoney has finally learned to be!

Could we but bank the beauty of our youth
And save it 'till our very ripest years...
Could Nature once reverse its path to truth
And teasing time dispel our dreadful fears...
Could passion burn its brightest at the last,
And its sweet pleasures fill our closing days...
What cheer we'd find when all our cares are past
And life is blessed with leisure's songful lays.
Then age would be the crown and paradise
Of all our labors, love and jostling joys.
Our passing hours topped with pungent spice
Would leave intact what time alone destroys.
    While lasting years may make us wise and strong
    Are we so sure that Nature has it wrong.

Each night I seek the peace that's found in sleep,
But then my mind proves traitor to my flesh.
The urgencies of other nights soon creep
Into my troubled thoughts to nightly etch
The memories of loving nights with you.
These images then race around my room;
A crucifying bitter sweet review
That shall haunt and taunt 'till I'm entombed.
If only I could close my eyes and dream
Of those very nights that we enjoyed.
At least the rest I'd find might somehow seem
A hint of hope, and not illusion's ploy.
    That heart is damned that knows not Lethe's art,
    The wisdom of forgetfulness comes tart.

Had I been blind from birth your beauty still
Would stir my heart with fancy's heated forms.
How then would touch enhance that tempting thrill
Your flesh excites whene'er I feel its warmth.
Your breath's the fragrance flowers imitate,
Your kiss the sweetest taste one could enjoy,
Your voice the song that angels emulate,
Your grace a swan-like dance demure and coy.
Bereft of eyes the mind finds visages
The other senses form for lack of sight.
The heart creates a world of images
That all deny its dark eternal night.
    Thus love will still enhance the human soul,
    For it alone may sense our being whole.

If I could be your true and perfect knight
I'd brave the world to win your wond'rous heart.
I'd master any task if you'd requite
My love. Your word is all I want to start.
What! you're not impressed by daring deeds.
You've never dreamed to win some hero's love.
You're horrified to learn some man would bleed;
Would risk his life—you hope it's all a bluff???
What qualities would you expect to find
In any lover? Wealth! An easy ardor!!!
How could I ever be so tot'ly blind.
How crude, uncouth, why did I even bother.
    I swear you make me feel that I've been used;
    It hurts to find one's self so misabused.

It seems I'm lord and owner of my face,
That false impression's pride's pure classic lie.
To leave what lies within without a trace's
The stoic's test—or vanity's reply.
A broken heart is not a pleasant sight;
The battle wounds of love leave quite a scar.
Were you to see my face in bed at night
You'd know the price I paid in Eros' war.
The face's fabrication's can't really hide
The pains a bad experience inspires.
Look closely then—you'll see what's hid inside
As plainly as some photo of hell's fires.
    The lacerations lover's earn are wounds
    They carry in their souls; and to their tombs.

No choir's canticles, no bells have rung
With that tranquillity your voice reveres.
A wistful silence sits upon my tongue;
The pregnant echo of my hopes and fears.
No hymns, no harmonies can catch the calm
Your words have woven on my loom of love.
In mute astonishment, quickquake alarm,
My senses reverberate my brain above.
This paradox of peace and passion mixed
In madness—divine madness—plays no jest.
Emotion's poles, transfigured and transfixed,
Transcend duality in fluid rest.
    Thus the more quietly you touch my soul....
    My flesh more quickly turns an embered coal.

ᴔ ?ᴔ

*O*blivion's a not unhappy lot.
It wears quite well even when ambition
Longs for more. Oh vanity has got
A valid claim or two if a worthy mission
Has quietly inspired one's wish for fame.
It's not that Epicurus has it wrong —
Still, stoic duties really have some claim;
A claim that's buttressed by a siren song.
A chosen life of Heraclean labor's
Better done in private. Its best reward's
The luck of being spared the bitter savors
Publicity affords to one who's toward.
    Hide the good you do beneath a basket,
    Renown is best attained from in a casket.

ᴔ ?ᴔ

*T*he warmth of winter's wines instills my thoughts:
I dream of summer days long since past.
My dormant mind recalls the works it wrought;
Its fledgling efforts—how else should such be classed?
My words cascaded forth in giddy tropes;
Consumed with longing desire was my theme.
Not only seamen need to learn their ropes;
I sought a tutor who'd teach this novice green.
Her tender lessons liquefy me still;
Its frothy vintage fructified with age.
Imparting arts with consummated skill
She calmly tempered passion's prickly rage.
    Though summer's heat has turned to winter's frost,
    While memories remain no warmth's been lost.

Were stars but servants to my eager will
And Nature mistress to my every whim
I'd bid that Tyrant Ancient's scythe be still...
That n'er a creature suffer Adam's sin.
The lambs would bed with lions, and beasts would feast
Upon the food of fantasy incarnate —
The leisure found in love would be the yeast
To store up treasures transcending fruits of fate.
Alas! the ordered orbs of heaven truants are
To my desires; seasons flow and ebb,
Their equinox of life and death's the bar
Of Destiny binding us to change's web.
    Can grace fulfill our hopes when Fortune fails
    And grant eternal life beyond the pale?

You say my verse is barren, out of date;
My metaphors are trite and quite old fashion.
Classical allusions no longer rate;
The erudite is ludicrous as passion.
Besides you hate the bounds of rigid form;
Poetry's not a science of mechanics.
Such lines as mine can't make a woman warm,
They're only fit to share with some pedantics.
You claim they're but a scholar's meager labors;
My sonnets smell of too much perspiration.
How could I ever hope to win your favors;
You're shamed to think you've been my inspiration.
    It's clear you think me rather quaint and antic;
    It's also obvious you're no romantic.

so ℰ so

𝒜 hollow echo whispers in my heart
The heaving to and fro of passion's bell.
My veins turned vibrant by desire's dart
Each tortured thought becomes a heaven-hell.
Affections flush, my brain in eager heat
Kindles the countless ecstasies we dared.
Each fusion of our flesh was bitter-sweet
With all the pleasure-pain our bodies shared.
Though time has turned against us I tremble still
To feel again those fantasies we knew.
Each effort to forget inflames my will
To keep alive a love that never grew.
    Condemned to crave a self-absorbing past;
    A haunted wraith while consciousness may last.

so ℰ so

𝒜re we but flesh and feeling devoid of Fate?
What mystifies our minds with doubt and hope?
Who can account for human love or hate;
Or who for life's labyrinths through which we grope?
It seems each day our destiny revives
Some inkling that the past transcends the tomb.
How often have we lived in other lives —
Were you Thais, Eloise, or whom?
What caused our hearts to throb? —some starker throes
Our souls inherited from darker shoals???
Were we two family, friends, or mated "foes"
Troth to play Eros' teasing obverse roles.
    My love is such I know we've loved before:
    And oft shall love again—again, and more!

Ecstasy's elixir lies upon your lips;
In every kiss I taste its luscious wine.
Bacchus' nectar pales besides these sips
Of joy that turned the god of war bovine.
I long to feel your flesh against my own
Embracing arms entwined. When passion's waves
Of love's sensations reverberate to bone
My mind grows mad with what my flesh still craves.
And when we're through I find the after shock
Has thoroughly consumed me heart and soul.
My sense of time belies the slavish clock
Because a night with you defies its toll.
     In loving you I've found a revelation
     That far exceeds religion's expectation.

How many incarnations have we shared;
Such love as ours can't grow in just one life.
A multitude of ages have prepared
Our hearts to alternate as man and wife.
In sequent matings we each have known the joy
That fleshly love accords to either sex.
When one would court the other would be coy;
The fate we share has held us in its hex.
Fools may scoff at this immortal magic,
But we could never doubt the soul's eternal.
How could we ever claim this life is tragic
When each return we've found our hearts are vernal.
     However oft' we've play this human game
     Its fascination's never quite the same.

I never met a woman I couldn't love,
And love with all my heart at least one night.
The plainest maids are diamonds in the rough;
For looks deceive. We trust too much to sight.
A prickly cactus lacks the rose's hue,
But how it glories in the sun's caress.
Far hardier it asks for little too,
Contented easily with happiness.
Though lovelier in charms the rose requires
A richer cultivation. Beneath its beauties
It holds a host of thorns that thwart desires
More oft' than cacti, for it's much too moody.
    My past has taught me finer sentiments:
    Love's fruits are found in kinder temperaments.

ᴚᴑ 𝒞 ᴑᴚ

I've had my share of womanly rejection;
A cross-eyed bald man's not a pretty sight.
It doesn't take an act of deep reflection
To understand the problems of my plight.
You know I'm not a man of noted wealth;
Nor have I any claim to worldly fame.
At least I'm spared those femme fatales of stealth
Who, maggot-like, will feed on men they tame.
What beauty's mine is hid beneath my hide,
And only seen by those who seek it there.
Yes, these defects do have a brighter side;
Those who do accept me sincerely care.
    While no Adonis, I'm loved for who I am;
    No better fate befalls a modest man.

45

⟡

*M*y mortal weakness is a woman's eyes;
A soulful look has often robbed my heart.
But should her eyes be filled with laughter why
My heart rejoices at what such eyes impart.
And should I see a twinkle that invites
Affection with a teasing sideways glance
My spirits leap with joy that such delights
Are in the offing however slight the chance.
No other tempting charms can quite equate
The subtle hint that lovely eyes convey.
A woman may remain serene, sedate;
But still her eyes will give her heart away.
     Yet eyes may lie as surely as the tongue;
     As all admit who ever have been stung.

⟡

*O*f course I'm carnal; what did you think I'd be?
Oh yes, I've hoped to win your heart—that's true.
That's not the only part that interests me;
You've other assets that attract me too.
There's nothing wrong with fleshly appetites,
Provided one indulges them with care.
I would not sleep where other's have their rights;
Somehow I doubt if that would be quite fair.
But you, my sweet, are most unspoken for;
As such we two should make a loving pair.
Why scruple over half forgotten lore,
Our youth's too precious to waste on ancient ne'ers.
     Let's bed together then, and damn the rest:
     If love's in doubt let feeling be the test.

⚬ & ⚬

*S*he was my senior by six or seven years;
Her face and figure both belied her age.
She'd tease me 'bout my youth; ("No beard appears
Upon your fuzzless face."). I was her page.
The Holy Rites of knighthood were her text;
I longed to be her new initiate.
She'd tempt me to the brink; she'd toy and vex
Until my loins would quake with love and hate.
She claimed her conscience keep her from the deed
That'd rob me of my eager innocence.
Oh, how I'd stalk about! I'd beg and plead,
And promise her some kingly recompense.
    My solemn page's vigil won at last
    A knight's reward to crown my virgin fast.

⚬ & ⚬

*T*he wind that blows along this desert waste
Is quick to blind us with our selfish fears;
Though love's sweet urge would bid us to make haste
Our foolish doubts succumb to ego's jeers.
That empty throne of thought's idyllic vales
Are verdant hopes that tease with phantom fruit;
But Eden's apple's future life's too stale
To tempt us from the present's sober truth.
We'll take the cash and let the credit slide;
Don't sell today to buy some unknown 'morrow.
We'll set our sail and trust the waiting tide
That floats us free beyond both joy and sorrow.
    When prophets prove their claim of what's to come
    We'll heed the call of ultrasonic drums.

＊ ℰ ＊

"To be or not to be..." that tortured thought
Has rippled through the shifting dunes of doubt
And sanded smooth what chiseled creeds have wrought;
Toppling pyramids of faith however stout.
No human tent of nothingness can stand
Against the howling force of hope-filled fear.
A caravan of questions reprimands
That conscience dogma turns upon its bier.
Rub the lamp of courage—its genie brings
The sacred prize that puzzles out the storm.
Resolution, facing chance undaunted, sings
The grace gratuitous from which our future's born.
    Let Fate spin Fortune's wheel how ere it will:
    Accept its challenge to be quick or still.

＊ ℰ ＊

We're of an age (I love your honesty!).
And yet it seems you dally in your youth.
I can't believe that you're as old as me —
Could it be you've not told me the truth!
You've hid the years others have to wear;
What tolls of time are there none can detect.
You claim it's 'cause your life's been free from care;
Perhaps that blessing does have this effect.
Why have I doubts: why my disposition?
I guess I must confess what's hard to bare.
You see I'm less inclined to enter in
An inter-generational affair.
    A would-be daughter's just too much to take:
    In playing daddy I'm sure I'd be a fake.

You say you see in me a laggard lover
Who's slow to sense the warmth a woman feels.
Perhaps the promptings love promotes in others
Have warned my wary heart before it reels.
An unredeemed romantic to the core
I can't contain the danger in my dreams.
Self deception's fooled me oft before;
No woman's quite as saintly as she seems.
Now disappointment dogs me, thus my doubts
Impede the path that passion's prone to take.
And yet my inner nature still will out
To pledge my bets and place my heart at stake.
　　Who can deny that love's an endless gamble,
　　But one who's lack leaves life a senseless ramble.

Against that time when you no longer care
I steel my heart with stoic meditations.
Aurelius is now my daily fare
To guard against Cronus' deprivations.
Against that time when nought but souvenirs
Are left to tell the tale of our affairs.
It's Epictetus' counsel I hold dear
For his advice in crisis never errs.
Against that time when your heart turns cold
Because it's learned to warm for someone else.
When star-filled eyes have finally seen I'm old
And fit for nought but prayer and vesper bells....
　　That time is sure to come so I must arm
　　Against the havoc of my heart's alarm.

⚘ 𝒞 ⚘

*A*s light inheres in air so God in thee;
He is the Soul that glorifies your flesh.
He grants the will that makes us mortals free,
However much our instincts move our mesh.
The mystery that magnetizes souls
And bonds them heart to heart is but His love.
This quality of life, enhanced and whole,
Enriches us with Being's treasure trove.
What cause have we to cry, or grieve, or fret,
To find ourselves the soil for other's seed.
That flesh may thrive on flesh as life on death
Fulfills us all through feeding someone's need.
    True love inheres in giving all we can:
    What better use have we for this our span.

⚘ 𝒞 ⚘

*B*lessed are they who bedded in their youth
May melt as one in mind, in heart, in flesh;
Who, joining pain with joy, create a truth
That's born unique with every child afresh.
Had we but preened and courted in our prime
To test the future's promise thorn and rose...
Could we reroll the roaring waves of time
That rush us onward toward our cycle's close...
Although the brevity of life allows
Our souls a single sip—let's taste the hope
That makes immortal all our present nows:
Eternalize each instant left our scope.
    The rarity of love is such a treasure
    It's worth the sport however short the measure.

so ℰ so

*H*ad some convent come to be my harem
Where every single nun's a virgin proved;
And every woman there's a lovely gem
Awaiting daily to become beloved.
Where each is starving more than all the others
To consummate her passion's one desire;
To have inflamed a heart her vows now smother
With all my manly presence may inspire.
Yet were this fantasy a living fact
I could not know a fifth of joy I've found
Embraced within your arms where every act
Of love inspires visions so profound
    That seraphims would sound their trumpets vainly
    To call me from your bed; and I speak plainly.

so ℰ so

I've never kept a woman in my life!
Nor have I ever frequented a house.
Untroubled sex that's tot'ly free from strife?
Well, you see, I'm just not that kind of louse.
Such sex is much too bland to suit my taste:
The simple act itself seems cold and raw.
It never works because it's merely waste:
Besides I'm sure it'd be an irksome bore.
I need passion's promptings to spark desire.
Oh, I admit it may be false illusion;
Nor is it something one may yet admire.
Since life's a lark so what if love's confusion.
    Who amongst us can live without his dream:
    There's too much pain in life to miss the cream.

so ℰ so

My mother grew a garden full of roses,
Which all my girl friends loved to get as gifts.
A dozen such with sonnet thus encloses
A sentimental gesture they loved to sniff.
There's nothing else can move a junior miss
With as much emotion or elation.
Those roses often won their sweetest kiss,
Which always caused a tingling sensation.
Alas, those simple days are long since gone,
And left their faded petals 'twixt life's pages.
And yet those memories still linger on...
Yes even now here in life's last stages.
   I sometimes laugh at all my boyhood ploys,
   But nothing since surpassed those teen-age joys.

so ℰ so

No loving incantations were more inspired
Than those I wrote for you. Too shy to tell
The passion that I felt I first desired
To find some way to place you in my spell.
I felt so sure that you'd politely say
You felt no interest, or that you loved elsewhere,
I had to steel my heart against that day,
Which made my secret love my constant care.
Though sonnet after sonnet sought some way
To tell my fears my love was too unsure.
I questioned every qualm, and then I'd pray:
Oh God! Provide me with some saving cure.
   At times I thought my poems were things of note:
   At times the ravings of a randy goat.

She was the sweetheart of my tender years
When I knew nought of love but boyhood dreams.
We were the best of friends, none were so dear
As she and I; we each wrote by the ream.
It seems that we exchanged a tome of verse,
Each poem exuberant with joy and hope.
In time we learned the art of being terse,
Our writings then attained a darker scope.
One day we each turned down a different path
To face our unknown fates in diverse ways.
Somehow the love we shared turned silent wrath —
We never met again until today.
    She lies there in her coffin cold and ashen,
    A body that had once burned hot with passion.

The many masks we wear to hide our hearts
Are false façades to serve the solitude
Our souls require to keep ourselves apart
From those who'd pry into each private mood.
For when our hearts are hurt we need to hide
The pain we feel from friend and foe alike.
However sad and weak we feel inside
We quell emotion's waves and plug the dike
That holds the tears we dread to shed or show.
How passion humbles pride's an ancient tale
That mortifies the minds of those who know
The curse of unrequited love's travail.
    The habits of my heart have proved too prone
    To love unwisely—it's not a thing unknown.

The wisdom of the heart's in water writ;
It changes ever with the ebb and flow
Of human passions, the poor moon's counterfeit,
Which first may hide in shadow, then may glow.
Alone again my heart's a thing of thirst;
My passion fails to rise, my pulse is slow.
The ache inside appears to be much worse —
To tell the truth I've never felt so low.
To find a fellow soul with loving eyes,
A tender heart, and magic in her voice.
Such a wonder could make my passions rise,
And teach my soul to once again rejoice.
  Love's not just some temporary craze;
  Much like the moon it flits from phase to phase.

We are the stuff of dreams; our own and those
Who love and cherish us. In sharing dreams
We share our souls. We share the common throes
Of life's eternal anarchy. The seam
That separates our egos joins and seals
Our hearts and hopes in one immortal bond.
What is a dream if not the heart's appeal
That man's existence exceeds this earthly pond.
Existence then becomes communion. We
Become the purest proof that there's a God.
This rounded sleep we share is meant to be
The testing time of this our mortal pod.
  Those multitudes who doubt the truth of this
  May never know how much their life's amiss.

54

What was it Bacon said about a wife
And children being hostages to fame.
His rival bested him at law and life;
Therefore, I doubt that Coke would think the same.
He may have lost the girl (and gold) to Coke,
But later took a lass he loved as true;
Yet all too oft' his debts would leave him broke.
His life's affairs had taught him then to rue
This marriage of the heart—at least where want
Of wealth dictates a prudent wiser choice.
As for his public life—he broke his bond
By taking bribes to sway his judge's voice.
    Thus disgraced his few remaining days
    Were spent in writing most of Shakespeare's plays.

Who can explain what motives move his mind
When all his heart is darkened with desire.
When love has left our senses sharp yet blind
Our thoughts and deeds are dead to reason's sire.
At best Apollo reigns but to the waist;
What lies below belongs in Bacchus' realm.
When love has proved but Aesop's bitter grapes
Then reason may regain our human helm.
Now that my passions have begun to cool
The dusk of our affair has finally dawned.
I knew you saw me as some stupid fool
When my ardor only made you yawn.
    I see my love's unsuited to your taste,
    And so my trust and travail's proved but waste.

A line of flick'ring candle tips Te Deums
Across the night that dwells within my mind.
This necrophantic troupe intones a paean
Of starkest silence whose echoes fright the blind.
A pallid Yorick's head appears.... it deigns
To coronate my cockiness with laughter;
And spurns these sheaves of vanity's refrains.
Its image haunts my heart with pride's disaster.
Sweet tarantula whose toxic kiss
Inundates my soul with dust's temptation.
The lust you've woven webs that gift of bliss;
Courage to join in death's reparation.
    We're nought except some unknown future's leaven;
    Men are always lent to life—never given.

⚜

Alas, my balding pate betrays my years
As plainly as the plainness of my face.
Thus never numbered 'mongst Adonis' peers
I'm never tempted past my modest place.
Ungodlike as I am I dare not dream
Of that impulsive love first sight bestows.
In truth I can't believe what surely seems
A gift of grace that caused your love to flow.
Can you really love this dune of dust;
This hapless home of sinew, bone and flesh.
You've seen my soul, you say, and therefore trust
My spirit's beauty's born each day afresh.
    Is love so blind or does it truly see
    The deeper being hid in mystery.

56

Ask not to find some likeness to my love;
She beggars those you place in her compare.
This angel's grace's a gift from God above;
And God n'er made her match—to that I'll swear.
Who can proclaim her charms? No poet would dare!
Nor any painter hope to raise his brush
To capture, if he can, her image rare —
For God alone can emulate her blush.
You'll note I never said a single word
To tell you what's she's like, or how she looks.
Or if her voice outsings the sweetest bird,
Or any mundane mark—like how she cooks.
    However much imagination soars
    It can't describe the one my heart adores.

Blind Nature knows nothing of our pain;
In league with Time it tortures us with doubt.
The two together make this world insane,
And drive us to the wall unless we're stout.
Darwinian dilemmas' darker deaths
Will plague our hopes throughout this mortal life.
When shall some specter come collecting debts;
For soon or late that piper's paid his mite.
We never know when our career shall close,
And so our souls must always be prepared.
When we receive that fatal blow of blows
We must not wince, or show that we are scared.
    A noble heart forestalls Death's fell arrest
    By bravely facing Fortune's restive test.

ᴖ ℰ ᴖ

Enjoy his art, but leave the man alone.
Analyze, criticize, do whate'er you will;
But most of all just enjoy his poems!
There's matter there to touch the heart and kill
Those unkindly urges to strip his soul
Of all its hidden secrets. Respect the man.
Have reverence for his genius given whole;
Be held in awe by all his sonnets' span
Of human passions and their mortal toll.
Those foolish academic crones; that clan
Of amateurs in life have no role
If prying into privacy's their plan.
    As Pope proclaimed, be a better bard;
    Try to emulate his skills however hard.

ᴖ ℰ ᴖ

My countenance's as sad as that old knight
Whom Sancho served in poor Cervantes' tale.
I've know his hopeless quest and mindless plight,
And shared his constant trials that always fail.
The windmills that I've lanced where women's beds;
For my illusions were as blind as his.
We each were lunatics who lost our heads
In gallant errantry for Dulcenia's kiss.
You seem to think that I'm that other Don,
The one of Mozart, Byron, and Molière.
It's nice to be so flattered, but when I'm gone
You'll see the truth, and not this false compare.
    The fallacies of fiction's claims to truth
    Are frauds that fool a dreamer who's too couth.

The chants of Gregory's even tempered grace
All voice the quiet calm of Christian faith.
Their rests and silences both fill the space
Enclosed by gothic stones of ancient date.
This pithiness of plain chant suits the style
Of anonymity those monks composed.
It venerates the Virgin even while
It leaves composers tot'ly undisclosed.
The music of the mass inspires all
Who truly feel its mystery's wonderment.
Though many come, how many heed the call
To raise their hearts proclaiming high intent.
    One soul alone leaves our eyes all glazed —
    Bach's B minor's the pinnacle of praise!

Scorn me not because I dare not say
A multitude of lover's lies. My mute
Impromptu moods vouchsafe I am but clay —
None else—and lack the angel's art at lute.
Trumpets never sound the silent truths
Vaulting souls' silent joys inspire.
Audacious words will never reach the roots
Love may lace with passion's dumb desire.
Earnest though I be I cannot voice
Non sequiturs to honest plain chant score.
Touched as I am my feelings must rejoice,
Intoning inwardly love's living lore.
    Notes but chime the calm while rests immerse
    Eternal trust in eager faith that's terse.

≫◦ 𝓔 ◦≪

The snows of yesteryear have come again
To blanket my illusions with their frost.
Their silent chill has stilled my heart, but then
They're just the residue of tempests tossed.
The sudden storm that ended our romance
Proved cyclonic in its destructive force.
Inside its eye I never had the chance
To change its path or circumscribe its course.
A momentary indiscretion's deed
Provoked the martyred passions you displayed.
The rose of our romance has learned to bleed,
And soured at its source our love's now frayed.
    If once we stray the straight and narrow path...
    Hell hath no fury like a woman's wrath.

≫◦ 𝓔 ◦≪

The wonder of the waltz enchanted us,
Its lovely liltings stole our hearts away.
We danced 'till dawn; its magic granted us
A treasured night of memories so gay.
In time we danced the tango, which hypnotized
Our hearts, and filled our eager flesh with flame.
My mind had never been so mesmerized;
I know my soul shall never be the same.
All I ever longed for seemed close at hand,
And when I sensed you shared these feelings too
Excited passion burned brighter than I'd planned.
You can't deny the ecstasy we knew!
    Don't let your doubts destroy this tender shoot:
    Our acorn holds an oak within its root.

When Durer's darkest horsemen ride again
And doom the world with their stark attack.
That great apocalypse of death and pain
Will place both high and low upon the rack.
For those who starve the slaughter will be slow;
While Death may linger less with those diseased.
The ones who fight will be the first to go;
The sword is swift and sure—it doesn't tease.
The few who might survive will be the worst;
They'll find themselves ensnared in living death.
They're the ones who'll know that they've been cursed;
These Sisyphoi will suffer with each breath.
    Who then shall care to be the first or last;
    For all shall share this common holocaust.

Your face and figure's purest Raphael
With lines so fine that Ingres might envy them.
Though Titian's hues may grace your citadel
Your features shine as bright as Rembrant's gems.
In me you see another poor El Greco.
Not so, you say? Perhaps not in the flesh.
My sad quixotic soul's not quite perfecto,
For heart and mind are still a muddled mesh.
Join together in a double portrait!
What artist should we ask to dare the deed?
Not Braque or Gris, no Cubist could relate
Our quaint illuminated lover's creed.
    The whole's some painted page from Holy Writ
    Whose composition calls for Tansey's wit.

So 𝒞 So

You've often hoped to have a perfect lover
Who sensed and satisfied your every whim;
Who somehow always knew and could uncover
Your secret shameless longings felt within.
You're sure there must be more to sex's surgings
Than your experience's so far revealed.
While still a virgin you imagined urgings
You know must still lie hid inside concealed.
May I suggest you try to feel these passions
With all your heart, and never with your head!
The brain is not the place you'll find the cash in
That gratifies the goings on in bed.
    You'll find that mind and matter meet and mesh
    More in an open heart than burning flesh.

So 𝒞 So

A love of quiet dignity's my style;
Maturer women of discerning taste.
To love a gentle heart may take awhile;
The heat of boyhood antics acts in haste.
Youth's violent passions quickly burn to ash;
The sudden death that's born of fancy's fuel.
Beware a false devotion, daring, brash;
The reckless residue of eager mules.
True affection needs the pregnant past
Experience alone provides us with;
For only loves of slow gestation last;
Such love alone may reach to passion's pith.
    While beauty eas'ly charms the callow youth,
    Personality's the prize for those with ruth.

Both Paul and Dante experienced a flash
That magnetized their minds upon the moment.
Their former loves became but dross and trash;
Their fates were sealed by their new-found atonement.
Each spent his span consumed with constant labors
To glorify his God, and spread His word.
Through epic and epistles now we savor
Those mysteries Tertullian thought absurd.
Unlike these blessed messengers of faith
I've never been enthralled upon the spot.
Not even first-sight love has tuned my fate;
Whatever gold I've gathered's turned to rot.
    No Beatrice's touched my heart to stir my soul,
    And if Damascus called it's left me cold.

Day by day we slowly join the ages,
Each another in our allotted span.
May Judgment place us then among the sages
To fill our part in His eternal plan.
A life of learning, love and service still
May never make amends for all our faults.
We pray for grace, and trust to heaven's will
We need not answer bail for blame's frail torts.
Our immortal longings would rest content
Were we among the shades in Dante's limbo.
Our covetousness to join that regiment
Surely's no sin to turn our fate akimbo!
    This humble plea's our modest hope's request;
    Some small abode among those semi-blessed.

Have you ever watched a woman from behind
And slowly followed her a block or two,
Avoiding passing her from fear you'll find
Her face and front were not the better view?
Have you ever sat in some secluded seat
Where others could not see that you were there
And watched then waiting, wond'ring who they'll meet;
And been entranced by their eyes or hair?
A woman's an amazing work of art
Much to be enjoyed as no others are.
Just watching them has oft' refreshed my heart,
And moved my muse even from afar.
    Imagination titillates the soul
    With subtleties, such seems to be its role.

I seem to feel the shadow of your soul;
Its sudden touch but hints eternity.
Its like some boundless sea whose waves all roll
Hypnotic'ly enhanced with mystery.
Both fear and wonder mate my mind in awe
To sense a love who's blessed with endless depth.
I find myself amazed, entranced, enthralled!
And left with numbing doubts I'm too inept.
How can I ever hope to reach the core
Your Being hides—it's life's most sacred trust.
Dare I dream my heart might yet explore
Your teasing paradox of human dust.
    With fervent prayer I quest your ghostly grail:
    And dread the consequence if e'er I fail.

Improper passion plagues me with desire;
It maddens me to think my love pure lust.
Yet who may judge when all inside's afire;
I hate to find my heart beyond all trust.
My reason's swamped by longing's tidal waves:
My sanity has lost its moorings too.
My mind rebels at being passion's slave,
And damns my flesh as false desire's glue.
Is this the price that's paid to humble pride:
That ego heretic who's sin is self.
Must we burn to ash the id inside
To resurrect a wiser sinless self.
    Are lover's beds all altars of cremation
    Where flesh melts into flesh in new creation.

My crown is in my heart, not on my head;
For majesty's a mental state in truth.
Since my age of pagehood my soul's been fed
Upon heroic deeds of noble youth.
My heart is regal, and so my thoughts are graced
With all that chivalry may still inspire.
Their play transforms the motley hues I've traced
And elevates them to a state that's higher.
My life's become a sacred odyssey
To add my mite to humanistic lore.
I'll stake my honor and my dignity
Upon the worth of all that I adore.
    Then humbly wait the fate that may be mine
    When God conjoins eternity with time.

Sidney said the surest way to write
Is from the heart, and only from the heart.
To pen the thoughts you've filched from former wrights
Makes craft seem cunning, and that's no way to start.
Such praise just complements the poet you quote,
And not the woman whom you wish to win.
Why make it seem as if you wrote by rote
When, where love's concerned, that's the gravest sin.
Just bow before the beauty who's your idol.
You'll find that silent awe's a certain choice
To tell your tongue is bound by Cupid's bridle:
Alive with love the best of poets loose voice.
    If other's words must serve to lisp your soul
    It's better far to borrow sonnets whole.

The connoisseurs of chaos are a crowd
Who revel in poetic liberties.
I've heard the verse of which these poets are proud
And find it doesn't do a thing for me.
My ear is not refined enough to catch
The subtleness of their sense or meter.
I've even tried to time it with my watch;
And found they've just scotched Paul to bolster Peter.
But then again I'm just an amateur
Who needs to have his lines go thump te thump.
Believe me when I write I make damn sure
My meters never miss a skip or bump.
    And should you find my sonnets are mere samples,
    It's 'cause I've robbed the Bard for my examples.

The mother's but the daughter decades hence,
And if she seems a sister at this time
It bodes quite well that aging's immanence
Shall alter slightly nature's gifts sublime.
Your mother's natural charm and sparkling wit,
Kindly warmth and quiet disposition
Are telltale signs you'll have that inner grit
To weather life's grueling inquisition.
I can't believe the interests that we share;
The gods could never grant a better fate.
I'm sure in bed we'll make a loving pair;
What more could one require of a mate?
    You're even good at chess—I'll take this rook.
    You've just one fault: I wish you'd learn to cook.

❧ ℓ ❧

The wounds of love that lacerate my heart
Are marks of honor, much like dueling scars.
The hurt each held, experience turned tart,
Became my bible in sex's holy wars.
When gambles of the heart would start again
My pulse would rise and race 'till gratified.
The bloodhound in my mind n'er missed the scent
Of luring lusciousness unsatisfied.
My rutting urge would fill my veins with verve;
All that mattered then were its demandings.
The explosive joys of ecstasy would serve
To bring a peace beyond all understanding.
    But then this taste of heaven turned to hell
    Until another temptress cast her spell.

༄ ❦ ༄

What did Plato know of Eros' joys?
He always lived amongst his ideal forms.
I doubt he even came to play with boys:
The cave of that convention was too warm!
The One Parmenides aspired to
Was his delight—Nous was all that mattered.
His trip to Syracuse then proved his rue;
Its philo-king wanted those who flattered.
This false disciple next betrayed his master
By making him a foolish comic butt.
Poor Socrates pre-escaped disaster
By taking hemlock. Oh, that unkind cut!
    Every Caesar has to have his Brutus;
    Still....post mortem patricide's the crudest.

༄ ❦ ༄

Yes, I've taken up with older women:
I just enjoy experience in bed.
My predilection's normal. Acumen's
More attractive when all is done and said.
Of course I feel some sympathy for virgins
Unschooled in Aphrodite's finer arts.
But teaching them's never been my burden —
I hate their pouts and tears, and bumbling starts.
They swear undying love—and then they blame
Everything in life upon their lovers.
When maturer women play the game
They tactfully leave faults beneath the covers.
    Why, madame, no, I'm not a gigolo.
    A necrophiliac? I don't think so.

Your grave's become a bed of highest honor
Because you gave your life in freedom's cause.
This sacrifice made you the noble donor
Of what's most dear—such courage gives one pause.
You lost a brilliant future playing sports:
You had been picked by baseball's premier team.
But Destiny had deigned to cut you short —
I never dreamed that Fate could be so mean!
In emulation I too joined the Corps,
And volunteered to put my life at risk.
I too have faced the darker dogs of war,
But Fortune spared me the Grim Reaper's kiss.
    Out there upon the ashen sands of Iwo
    I lost my dearest friend: a fallen hero.

Bring forth those paladins of chivalry;
Arthur, Igor, Roland, and El Cid:
Bid each prepare to meet his calvary —
These epic heroes I'd conquer for a quid.
Have Merlin conjure up hell's evil horde;
Mammon, Beial, Beelzebub, et al:
I'll make them bow before our martyred Lord —
Or plague them all with ills that would fret Paul.
Not least of all confront me with seduction;
Let Helen, Circe, even Eve herself,
Tempt me with luring charms and lustful sin —
I'll prove pure Galahad, true blue loyal Guelph.
    Imagining such feats is so exhausting
    I've hardly energy for love's sweet tossing.

Decade after decade Petrarch's peers
Have plied their trade until this very day;
In sonnet after sonnet shedding tears
For unrequited love, some virgin's nay.
Each woman that they woe's a wife and mother
Whom honor, faith and pride have all kept distant.
They swear their love is true, they'll have no other;
Upon this point their poems remain insistent.
In truth these troubadours are held in awe
By the Virgin Mother. Others are at most
Mere manikins her model's underscored —
All false and fleshly Holy Grails and Hosts.
    And yet this modern world's medieval minds
    Retain their magic to make lovers blind.

Falling sparrows, ordained by destiny
To live some little lot of measured time.
We're screeching gulls who sense the mystery
Of reddened dawns....who drown too soon in brine.
Illusion's eagles, who think we rule the skies,
We're doomed to share the fate of dodo birds.
Not a jay among us, howe'er he lies,
Has art enough to conquer death with words.
Immersed in passion's fledgling paradox
We flutter through and fro on waves of air.
We build a world composed of nests and flocks
Untroubled by the stiffened form's vacant stare.
    A warden hawk awaits his chance to swoop;
    The moment strikes! and calls us from this coop.

Her grace was liquefaction head to toe,
The ease with which she moved belied ballet.
It seemed her form would dance and face would glow
With angelic elegance and impish play.
And yet I saw such sadness in her eyes
I wondered at the loss that left it there.
Of course I never asked — I never pried —
But still it bothered me the more we paired.
There comes that point when lovers all reveal
The troubles they have hidden in their past.
She told me then that she could never feel
Enough for me to ever make it last.
    Her only love was killed back in the war —
    She knew she'd never love another more.

My errant herald's eager embassy
O'er steps his station in shooting Cupid's darts.
He's sent to parley not lay siege for thee
To drop the drawbridge to your fortress heart.
This fool has fancied he's some ancient knight
Who braves the topless towers of countless Troys.
What quixotic nonsense! — windmills the like
Of crumbling castles built in sand by boys.
Illusion's lance lies broken; it's pennant's furl
Droops in leaden alchemy. Yet, hear his plea...
His faith has hope if Helen's face can hurl
Achaean fleets across a wine dark sea.
    Thy beauty's charm transmutes all baser minds:
    Once dubbed by thee he stands a nobler kind.

No other appellation's quite as fine
As that of friend. It oft' bespeaks a bond
Between two men that ages well as wine.
The sexes share a love that goes beyond
This sense of brotherhood. It complements
Divided nature's need to procreate.
But brotherhood's the mirror supplement
That gives a man a goal to emulate.
How incomplete our lives would be without
A friend's affection. Nothing else fulfills
Our souls as finding friends who prove as stout
As battle tested loyalty ever will.
    The trinity of God, and mate, and friend's
    The partnership of love that's life's sole end.

Oh how she loved to lay-a-bed with men;
She had a pleasing sweet seductive way.
Her touch electrified one's flesh, and then
She'd tease awhile before she'd softly play.
The afterglow her loving gave one's heart
Brought untold peace, and yet enticed one on.
How eagerly I'd seek another start —
Her patience never flagged when all was gone.
How proud I was: I stood so straight and tall
In thinking I alone possessed her charms.
But when my greedy heart demanded all,
She found another fool to fill her arms.
    This Circe's made each man a lusting cur:
    But God, it was so good to sleep with her.

Prophet, priest, and poet: all three am I.
For I evoke the images that find
The soul's eternal source. The trade I ply
Predicts the form and future of the mind.
Accursed or blessed these defter verbal strokes
Cut swift and deep. This mental samurai's
A dedicated monk whose prayers evoke
The God that lies within who never dies.
To cut the ego to its very core
Requires words whose music echoes all
The reverence the prayers of prophets score.
Is not the poet's voice the muezzin's call?
    No wonder Plato feared us poets the most:
    We touch the soul as does the Holy Ghost.

ᴏ ℰ ᴏ

The music of your voice still resonates
Inside my mind long after I've come home.
But since we've only met I hesitate
To call and keep you speaking on the phone.
Melodic modulations of your voice
Have reached into my heart impeaching sleep
With music much like madrigals by Boyce
To turn my room into a choir keep.
I wonder when we'll ever meet again,
And feel some fear you might be spoken for.
I readily admit I seem insane;
Yet sense in you a someone to adore.
    Thus smitten so I send this single rose,
    A humble token wrapped in rhyming prose.

The sonnet first was sung in Sicily;
Lentino wrote it then in Frederick's court.
What went before remains a mystery;
Some think it was a troubadouric sport.
Soon after Dante made this poem more pensive,
And Petrarch pleaded for his perfect love.
Other tongues then made the form extensive
Across the continent, below, above.
In Henry's time Wyatt made it englished;
In Bess's age William gave it form.
Then Donne and Milton made it more distinguished;
And in my way I've tried to make it warm.
    So if I have a slight Sicilian flare
    It's though a distant son my roots are there.

We live in troubled times when threats of war,
And war itself, obsess our hearts and minds.
The deaths of loved ones stirs us to the core,
As day by day we face the future blind.
Though desperate hope gives way to outright fear
We struggle on anxious though we be.
We ask in all our prayers, "Preserve our peers."
And long for loved ones far across the sea.
We'd gladly give our life in fair exchange
For a lover, friend or kin who's in harms way.
That peaceful past we knew now seems quite strange
So keen's the urgency that is today.
    What's in our hearts feels both unreal and real,
    Except when we're too numb to even feel.

Yes, secretly I sonneteered for him;
He could not voice his feeling with his pen.
To help a friend in need's no mortal sin.
Faced with the choice I'd gladly 'sin' again.
The thoughts were his, I only lent the words;
How often have you borrowed from a friend.
You think I love you! The very thought's absurd.
Betray a friend for love—may God forfend!
My feelings were not fraudulent, that's true;
Nor ever where they personal, I swear.
Admittedly I could feel love for you,
But reason rules my heart in this affair.
    Of course I value honor more than love:
    Minds have passions hearts know not of.

Your looks are sparks igniting passion's fuel,
Engulfing me with infernal fires.
Confusion reigns where the mind should rule
Because my thoughts betray my heart's desires.
I sense your eyes have hinted that tonight
Undreamed of love shall cause my soul to soar
Beyond the furthest galaxies in sight!
Yet when we're through I'll beg again for more.
The aura you exude's a subtle glow
That shows you feel as strongly as I do.
You can't imagine how my longings grow
In contemplation of this night with you.
    Why waste our date in conversation when
    A night of love awaits to prompt my pen.

so ? so

*A*ll I ask is just a simple grave,
A sack, a box of pine, a celtic cross,
Not unlike the ones Carthusians have;
That I was not a monk became my loss.
The more one knows the vanity of speech
The more one sees the need for total silence.
The love of calm and quiet Carthusians teach
By their example becomes the valence
That bonds the order each to each, and to God.
This world of words is just a place of pride;
Of empty vanity—we think our poems a pod
Of beauty; a beacon others use as guide.
    Must we lay beneath the sod to see
    Ecclesiastes speaks to you and me.

so ? so

*C*all me a slave to passion if you will;
Think me a fool who lacks all common sense;
Remind me life has other joys that thrill;
Insist the Fates will claim their recompense.
There's nothing you can say I did not tell
Myself a dozen times before I knew
The joy of loving her. Perhaps some hell
Awaits when our affair is finally through.
Why then I'll face that hell, and face it gladly.
Let all the Fates then curse me—I don't care!
I love her madly, do you hear, quite madly.
Whatever love may cost I'll pay the fare.
    Without her love my life has lost its ruth:
    Her loss leaves me a walking corpse in truth.

Farewell, sweet love, go trouble other hearts;
Go tease your way into another's bed.
Of cheap deceptions I'll have no further part;
You've never truly meant what you have said.
You take delight in all your little lies
As if the truth's some children's make-up game.
The fibs you fabricate leave sense defied!
You'll never change — you'll always be the same.
I never dreamed you played so fast and loose:
At first I trusted you — was I *that* blind?
When caught outright you give the same excuse:
A woman has a right to change her mind.
    You've cheated me of truth just once too often:
    Before we love again I'll corpse a coffin.

Hermes, god of thieves and tradesmen, iron
My nerve and help me steal her heart. No chaste
Artemis shall bind me as Orion
In some platonic love affair to waste.
Hephaestus, god of fire, help me forge
Desire's golden net to snare her flesh.
Hera's pride shall never by my scourge
While Odysseus' wit in me is fresh.
Orpheus, together let us charm her soul
And raise her up from Pluto's lucre — Hades.
With song and sonnet let us scribe her scroll
Surrendering Parnassus to the maid.
    Aphrodite, love's apothecary,
    Make us ever happy, never wary.

How sad the rose who grows among the weeds
With no companion of her hue or kind.
Her life a drudge she dreams to drop her seeds
In fertile ground, the finest she can find.
She longs to share a lovely garden where
A host of roses grows on every stem;
And where no weeds reside because of care
The gardener takes to breed and nourish them.
You are that rose who's languished much too long
In fields unfit for such a gentle flower.
You need a man who's love is true and strong
To come and make your bed a joyful bower.
    You are the stuff of dreams, and soon you'll be
    A rose who revels in reality.

In younger days I faced the threat of death
On more than one occasion. Somehow it
Never seemed quite so near to fear its breath.
Was it the youth's refusal to admit
One's mortality? Or was it just naive
Innocence—the eager youth's bravado.
Perhaps I simply never could believe
That God would ever end my life staccato.
Alas, I'm older now by many years...
I've learned that life's a truly lovely gift
I took for granted. Yes, I've learned to fear
Its loss from friends of whom I'm now bereft.
    Death comes upon us in a double guise:
    The loss of loved ones teaches us to die.

꜀ꙩ꜀

My heart's as scarred as some torero's thighs,
For Cupid gores as deep as any bull.
No lover suffers less when his flesh dies
To have his passions practiced to the full.
The pain's as fresh each time no matter how
One tries to salve his wounds with newer love.
For years I've only lived for here and now,
Believe me carpe diem's not enough.
The cairns of my affairs are graveyard stones
That stretch beyond infinity and back.
Each laceration cut right to the bone
Where self esteem endures the ego's flack.
    This civil war of self exacts a carnage
    That surely must be worse than marriage bondage.

꜀ꙩ꜀

The specs of light that swirl about the skies
Are gaseous sands that form a beach of suns.
Come, let our meditations mesmerize
Their astral vertigo into Cupid's fun.
Let us frolic on this spiraled strand
Oblivious to the oceanic void
That lies beyond: its unknown tides command
This universe created or destroyed.
Those fools of faith who trust in judgment are
An endangered species of desperadoes.
They're Pride's accountants who play chess with stars
And dread the dice that dance around their haloes.
    Evil exists! for those who think it must:
    The brave accept whatever comes with trust.

꙳ 𝒞 ꙳

𝒯here is a paradox that plagues my mind.
Were I pure thought what freedom I would gain
From those limitations our bodies bind.
But would I also then be free from pain?
And would I also then be free from love!
To what extent is loving bound to flesh?
Can love exist in some more spectral stuff
Or must it have the senses' tempting mesh?
Can a disembodied mind bring content?
Do the joys and pains the flesh provides
More than compensate the mind's lament?
Perhaps the passions are our truest guide.
    Would Platonic love prove to be the best:
    Or need we bodies to fulfill love's quest?

꙳ 𝒞 ꙳

𝒲e live with half our hearts in here and now
Attending to the daily chores of life.
The other half's more heavenly endowed
To search life's multiverse in spite of strife.
Exploring avenues however harsh
Imagination's magic fuses fact
With fancy, and finding fiction all too sparse
It questions constantly its very lack.
Still we think us richer far than those
Drones and churls who run this crazy world.
They swear that poets are poor and insane souls
Because their tainted mundane spirits' furled.
    They prize the scope and limit of their wit
    N'er knowing keener joys more infinite.

When I am buried dust my ghost shall groan
In recollection of these nights with you.
I'll long to feel my manly flesh and bone
Arise again to love with you anew.
Each time I die enfolded in your arms,
I die in hope of mortal resurrection.
The sheer delight enjoying all your charms
Has shown my soul approaches pure perfection.
I weep to think our senses slack with age;
Admittedly this life is only lent.
No wonder now my heart is racked with rage
To think a time will come when passion's spent.
    A sexless heaven's just another hell
    Until my dust turns flesh that feels your spell.

Why no, I'm not some subtle Casanova
Who only wants to get you into bed.
How often have I told you I'm no rover;
I'm faithful to my love whatever's said.
Of course I've been involved with other women;
You hardly think a man my age untried.
You wouldn't want a man who wasn't human;
Of this you may be sure—I've never lied.
I've never promised anyone in vain.
I'll keep my word until the heaven's fall.
With all my heart I mean the things I claim;
If you think I'm bluffing, raise or call.
    No. I can't account for some tomorrow;
    Who knows if it may hold our joy or sorrow.

ɔ·ɛ·ɔ

Yesterday's temptation's all seem stale now:
Those gulling witches offered untold glory!
Yet, without issue their promises are pale now:
Unpurposed passion's bitter taste just bores me.
Their ghostly shadows pass before my eyes
As one by one they fade beyond my tomb;
Their haunting echoes stir my heart to cry...
Aware their cackling sounds the crack of doom.
Though barren Death may knell his patient watch
Hear it not, but heed my supplication.
Choke laughing bitches by whom hope was scotched,
And mate our flesh in love and replication.
   Each child shall join our present joy and sorrow
   Tomorrow, and tomorrow, and tomorrow.

ɔ·ɛ·ɔ

Your love has been my Holy Resurrection;
My soul was dead, my flesh a walking corpse.
With one reviving kiss your sweet perfection
Defeats the Darker Ghost of all he thwarts.
With you the play of love's a mystic act
From which I rise ecstatic as a saint.
That love transforms the soul's a proven fact;
Who can deny true love will never taint.
If your embrace is not angelic then
I fear that somber host might have his day.
Yet, blessed with burning passion who cares when
That stealthy specter comes to claim his clay.
   If this be sin our love has been as vain
   As any heretic's consumed by flame.

A tired sun sinks out of sight;
Its day's work done it goes to rest.
Dusk descends then turns to night;
Its colors blend in mingled quest.
Through shadowed forms they search they sky;
But soon are torn as thought unbuoyed.
They're cast aside and left to die;
For night abides in endless void.
With silent voice night seems to tell
The deep rejoice it brings the whole.
Its quiet charm, its soothing spell;
Are like a psalm that fills the soul.
    Then dawn appears with rosette rays,
    The darkness clears though silence stays.

Auburn rose of autumn, winter's come
To press between your petals virgin snow.
Those sanctioned celibates would render numb
Your verdant springs from which sweet life may flow.
Why court a fallow fame that fades with years
And leaves your beauty minted cold on coins?
Love stays the sister's scissor hand who sears
The tread you weave on looms beneath your loins.
Not sterile sands but seeds slip down the curve
Of gracious time contained within your glass.
These potent grains shall make the sickle swerve
That Fates ordained may pray no funeral mass.
    For fruitful flesh will prove your body's tomb
    'Till heaven's host sends harbingers of doom.

Forever mortal, yet forever young,
The human core and crown of patient earth.
Too forgetful of soil from which you've sprung
You give this passing life eternal worth.
You hope, you dream, you dare, and from your mirth
You build your truth and gloss it with your tongue.
You make yourself a god by giving birth
To self deceiving pyramids of dung.
In your success there lies a haunting pain;
A mocking jest, a bitter taste of power.
In grasping all what can you hope to gain....
Gathered fruit scattered at the naked hour.
    Molded form. risen from the planet's crust;
    A moment's pause, and you retreat to dust.

I dreamt myself a corpse as cold as ice;
A horrid sight and most unlovely view.
Thus fit for nought except a meal for mice
My face and flesh were maggot's meat to chew.
All creatures share this common lot I know;
None may default this destined recompense
The pendulum of Nature's vertigo
Exacts from each before we go from hence.
Awake I search the depths within your eyes
To find another fate awaits me where
My being's essence dares refute this guise
Denying nightmare's stark and vacant stare.
    Such love as yours most surely must transcend
    All mortal musings that mystify our end.

so ❦ so

I swear my ghost will nightly haunt your bed
If you should scorn me now while love burns so.
Unrelieved by you I'll soon be dead
And gone where unrequited lovers go.
Then from that dark hereafter where death's spent
I'll come and curse your lovers 'till they're cold.
I'll make them impotent 'till they relent
And leave. You'll grieve for me until you're old.
But should you find me fit for your embrace
There're no delights we could not share together.
I promise you that daily we'll both face
A sunny life however foul the weather.
   The choice is yours now that you've been forewarned:
   No hate can equal that of lovers scorned.

so ❦ so

My soul has gnawed the bone of nothingness;
It's famished for the food of mystic faith.
It longs to be among the saintly blessed,
Yet lacks the grace it hungers to instate.
Its very emptiness painfully explores
Those silent powers it suspects exist
To furnish nourishment and end these wars
Where damning doubts ravishingly persist.
And though my starving spirit's bowed in prayer
It's too ashamed to ask for sustenance.
Its worthless merits make it well aware
Its loss of trust deserves no recompense.
   If justice reigns divine I know too well
   I'm doomed to join the hordes in Dante's hell.

Quite rightly think that I'm a loathsome lover.
But not for all the world would I dare tell
Your charms in public praise. Fools uncover
Their beloved's beauties. I know too well
The price that's paid when all and sundry see
Such priceless qualities as you alone
Possess. Believe me, dear, I'm not that crazy.
I fully mean to keep you for my own.
Write you a private sonnet then? Perhaps.
It's not a task I relish; not a bit.
Your charm's pure gold; and words are merely scraps.
Quite honestly the fact's I lack that wit.
     What Lao Tze said of God is true of you;
     No words can tell the Ultimate Taboo.

The door of darkness always stands ajar
Inviting us to pass beyond its portals.
It knows us for the fragile things we are;
Its fears and fascinations tempt us mortals.
A world of Hamlets waiver on the edge;
Both dreams and doubts disturb their peace of mind.
Imagination proves their potent wedge
To pierce that emptiness that leaves us blind.
Foreseeing realms of joy and realms of pain
The madd'ning puzzle never seems to cease.
Thus death's dilemma ever stays the same;
At least oblivion provides eternal peace.
     With stoic courage seize the day of fate:
     They also die who only stand and wait.

>&ℓ&<

The painful gnawing impotence I feel
In wanting to ease your every sorrow
Plagues me with shame! Nothing else seems real
Except these longings stirring in my marrow.
Kindness and compassion are all I have
To offer—my ascetic way of life
Has left me with nothing more to give save
Myself, and my struggles with my own strife.
Until luck inspires fortune's turning
All I can hope to grant is empathy.
Still, you could relieve my helpless yearning
If you graciously accept my sympathy.
    Though blessed to give, however small the stake;
    At times it's far more blessed for one to take.

>&ℓ&<

The time has come for us to say "Adieu",
For love has turned autumnal. Soon the frost
Will turn its varicolored foliage blue
As ice—then leave our love a leaf embossed.
This sad memento's pressed upon the page
Our passions authored while excitement surged.
When love enjoyed its warming summer stage
It seemed so true…yet proved a passing urge.
Try as I may I can't explain our change
Of heart. Can you? I know you feel the same;
You've changed as much as I—it seems so strange;
Although I know we neither bear the blame.
    When love's allurements all have finally died
    We best confess the loss and part with pride.

Those cursed ticks that clock us through this life
Are traitors all to immortality.
They toll the doubts with which our days are rife
With death's mechanic punctuality.
A possibility that's passed becomes
The cairn that marks a much too cautious mind;
Unmoved hearts remain forever numb;
Unsighted souls remain forever blind.
Be not deaf to our too numbered hours;
They plead as I to consummate our love.
Bow before those ever potent powers
Bestowed upon us to recreate our love.
    A sadder consummation only stays
      Upon the second hand that seals our days.

What lies within my heart surpasses show,
Nor can some magpie muse parade my mind.
There are some truths the heart alone may know,
And what's hid there no words may ever wind.
Within the quiet close of my poor soul
Resides a love that shall defy the worms
Of time that hunger for this humble scroll
Of mine that harbors all my heart affirms.
Nor will soliloquies ere sonnet forth
The contents that I closet in my heart.
However much my passions may exhort
My voice remains immune to Cupid's dart.
    To learn what's there requires time and trust
      And lacking that none get beyond my crust.

Zeus was such a bashing bore in bed;
He always slept with women only once.
They'd never have him back beneath their spread
Because he was as dull as any dunce.
Whatever form he took he was a bull
Whose only thought was how to probe his pleasure.
Any night with him proved one long lull
From which relieving sleep would be a treasure;
Except this proto-Kong would play the ape
Who after orgasm bellowed regnant.
Indulging often in olympic rape
He always left his victims all too pregnant.
    His antics made their lives a total wreck;
    Besides, so few enjoyed it a la Grec.

A decade hence when you again may read
The words here writ to fill an idle hour
I hope that you'll have found the truths they plead
Becoming more and more your private dower.
Our flesh has much to teach us that our minds
May only grasp when tutored by our hearts.
For love's a motley mix of many kinds
And comes upon us oft in fits and starts.
They are most blessed who find a love that lasts;
A love that's fruitful to the very end.
But oft what's prologue soon becomes what's past;
Although with luck we still may have a friend.
    Whatever Fate affords I wish you well;
    And all the love that words can never tell.

꘎ ℓ ꘎

Index of First Lines

so ȹ so

SEQUESTERED SOLILOQUIES
was designed by Bruce Sager
and typeset by Mary Trovato
of The Image Foundry
Baltimore, Maryland
in December of 1993.

The typeface family
BETH LIGHT
was employed in the production
of this book.